Music Minus One Vocals

2125

Professional Sound Tracks

Vol. 5

BROADWAY

Professional Sound Tracks

BROADWAY

CONTENTS

Some Enchanted Evening

Words and Music by
Richard Rodgers & Oscar Hammerstein II

This Nearly Was Mine

Words and Music by
Richard Rodgers & Oscar Hammerstein II

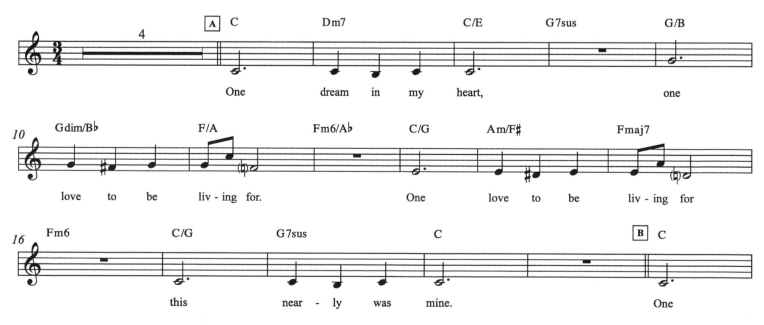

MMO 2125

Oh, What A Beautiful Morning

Words and Music by
Richard Rodgers & Oscar Hammerstein II

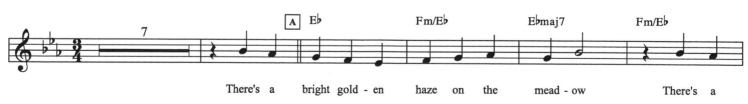

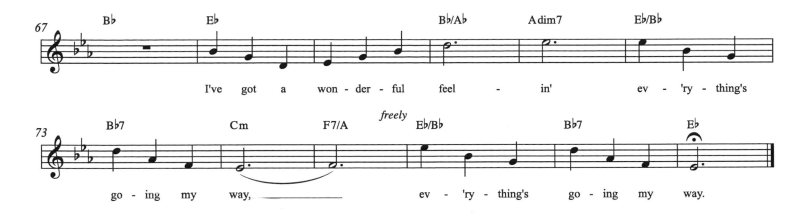

I've got a won-der-ful feel-in' ev-'ry-thing's go-ing my way, _____ ev-'ry-thing's go-ing my way.

Surrey With The Fringe On Top

Words and Music by
Richard Rodgers & Oscar Hammerstein II

Chicks and ducks and geese bet-ter scur-ry___ When I take you

out in the sur-rey,___ When I take you out in the sur-rey with the fringe on

top! Watch that fringe and see how it flut-ters___ When I drive them

high step-pin' strut-ters!___ Nos-ey folks 'll peek thru' their shut-ters and their eyes will

pop! The wheels are yell-er, the up-hols-t'ry's brown The dash-board's gen-u-ine

leath-er, With i-sin-glass cur-tains y' can roll right down, In case there's a change in the

MMO 2125

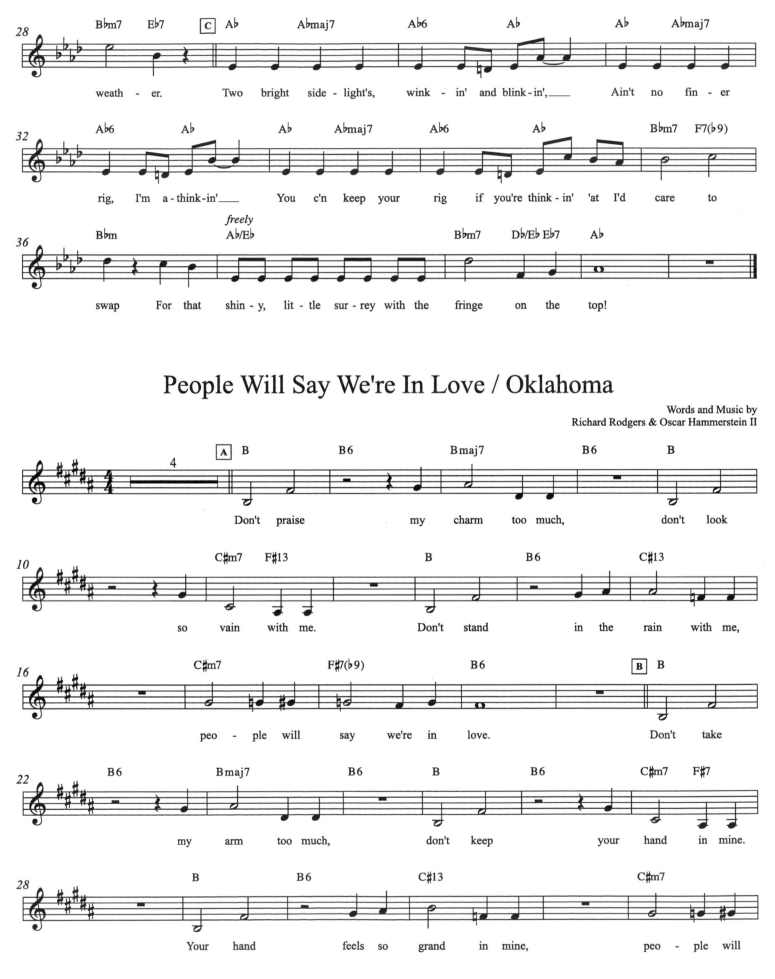

People Will Say We're In Love / Oklahoma

Words and Music by
Richard Rodgers & Oscar Hammerstein II

Memory

Words and Music by
Andrew Lloyd Webber

I Won't Send Roses

Words and Music by
Jerry Herman

(Where Do I Begin?) Love Story

Words and Music by
Carl Sigman & Francis Lai

MMO 2125

Send In The Clowns

Words and Music by
Stephen Sondheim

Other Great Vocals from Music Minus One

Professional Sound Tracks, Vol. 1 ....MMO 2121
In The Still Of The Night • The Very Thought Of You • As Time Goes By • Yours • My Foolish Heart • I'll Be Seeing You • Harbour Lights • Red Sails In The Sunset

Professional Sound Tracks, Vol. 2 ....MMO 2122
The More I See You • Stardust • Moonlight Becomes You • I'm Getting Sentimental Over You • A Lovely Way To Spend An Evening • Long Ago And Far Away • I Don't Want To Walk Without You • You Belong To My Heart

Professional Sound Tracks, Vol. 3 ....MMO 2123
Embraceable You • I Wish I Knew • I'll Walk Alone • You'll Never Know • They Say It's Wonderful • Born Again • So In Love • The Girl That I Marry

Professional Sound Tracks, Vol. 4 ....MMO 2124
They Say It's Wonderful • My Defenses Are Down • Why Do I Love You? • Make Believe • Old Man River • If Ever I Would Leave You • Don Quixote (Man of La Mancha) • Dulcinea (Man of La Mancha) • The Impossible Dream (Man of La Mancha)

Professional Sound Tracks, Vol. 5 ....MMO 2125
Some Enchanted Evening • This Nearly Was Mine • Oh, What a Beautiful Morning • Surrey With The Fringe On Top • People Will Say We're In Love /Oklahoma • Memory • I Won't Send Roses • (Where Do I Begin) Love Story • Send In The Clowns

Professional Sound Tracks, Vol. 6 ....MMO 2126
I Only Have Eyes For You • You Go To My Head • Autumn In New York • My Funny Valentine • Am I Blue • I Don't Know Why (I Just Do) • You Took Advantage Of Me • I Cover The Waterfront • Someone To Watch Over Me

Night Club Standards, Vol. 1 (Female) ....MMO 2131
The More I See You • It Had to Be You • The Shadow of Your Smile • Watch What Happens • The Good Life • Call Me Irresponsible • Street of Dreams • I Should Care

Night Club Standards, Vol. 2 (Female) ....MMO 2132
They Can't Take That Away From Me • Come Rain Or Come Shine • Nice 'N' Easy • That Old Black Magic • It's Only A Paper Moon • Summer Wind • The Very Thought Of You • I Left My Heart In San Francisco

Night Club Standards, Vol. 3 (Female) ....MMO 2133
I've Got The World On A String • Saturday Night (Is The Loneliest Night Of The Week • It's De-Lovely • Something's Gotta Give • Where Or When • Witchcraft • I Thought About You • Without A Song

Night Club Standards, Vol. 4 (Female) ....MMO 2134
The Best Is Yet To Come • I Could Have Danced All Night • They All Laughed • Oh, Look At Me Now • If I Had You • I'm Old Fashioned • A Nightingale Sang In Berkeley Square • The Lady Is A Tramp

The Great Ladies Of Jazz, Vol. 1 ....MMO 2135
A Good Man Is Hard To Find • Guess Who's In Town • Rockin' Chair • A Hundred Years From Today • It Don't Mean A Thing • Lullaby Of The Leaves • Goody Goody • Guess Who I Saw Today • What Is This Thing Called Love? • Moments Like This

The Great Ladies Of Jazz, Vol. 2 ....MMO 2136
Take The 'A; Train • Million Dollar Secret • Day Dream • Cried For You • Maybe • Too Late Now • Peel Me A Grape • Blue Gardenia • Street of Dreams • All That Jazz

Other Great Vocals from Music Minus One

Vol. 1 - Sing the Songs of George & Ira Gershwin..................................MMO 2101
Somebody Loves Me • The Man I Love • Bidin' My Time • Someone To Watch Over Me • I've Got A Crush On You • But Not For Me • S'Wonderful • Fascinatin' Rhythm

Vol. 2 - Sing the Songs of Cole Porter.............................MMO 2102
Night And Day • You Do Something To Me • Just One Of Those Things • Begin The Beguine • What Is This Thing Called Love • Let's Do It • Love For Sale • I Get A Kick Out Of You

Vol. 3 - Sing the Songs of Irving Berlin.........................MMO 2103
Cheek To Cheek • Steppin' Out With My Baby • Let's Face The Music And Dance • Change Partners • Let Yourself Go • Say It Isn't So • Isn't This A Lovely Day • This Year's Kisses • Be Careful, It's My Heart

Vol. 4 - Sing the Songs of Harold Arlen ....MMO 2104
I've Got The World On A String • Down With Love • As Long As I Live • Stormy Weather • I've Got A Right To Sing The Blues • The Blues In The Night • Out Of This World • Come Rain Or Come Shine • My Shining Hour • Hooray For Love

Vol. 5 - Sing More Songs by George & Ira Gershwin, Vol. 2 ....MMO 2105
Of Thee I Sing • Embraceable You • Oh, Lady Be Good • How Long Has This Been Going On? • Summertime • Love Walked In • Nice Work If You Can Get It • I Got Rhythm

Vol. 6 - Sing the Songs of Duke Ellington ....MMO 2106
Do Nothin' Until You Hear From Me • I Got It Bad (And That Ain't Good) • I Let A Song Go Out Of My Heart • It Don't Mean A Thing (If It Ain't Got That Swing) • Mood Indigo • Solitude • Sophisticated Lady • Don't Get Around Much Anymore

Vol. 7 - Sing the Songs of Fats Waller ....MMO 2107
I'm Gonna Sit Right Down And Write Myself A Letter • I've Got A Feeling I'm Falling • Squeeze Me • S'posin' • Two Sleepy People • Ain't Misbehavin' (I'm Savin' My Love For You) • Honeysuckle Rose • I Can't Give You Anything But Love • It's A Sin To Tell A Lie

Vol. 8 - Sing the Songs of Cole Porter, Vol. 2 ....MMO 2108
You're The Top • Easy To Love • Friendship • Anything Goes • Blow, Gabriel, Blow • You're The Top (Jazz Version) • I Get A Kick Out Of You • Anything Goes (Jazz Version)

Vol. 9 - Sing the Songs of Jimmy McHugh ....MMO 2109
It's A Most Unusual Day • You're a Sweetheart • Don't Blame Me • I Feel A Song Coming On • I'm in the Mood for Love • I Can't Give You Anything But Love • I Can't Believe That You're in Love with Me • On the Sunny Side of the Street • I Must Have That Man

Vol. 10 - Sing the Songs of Jerome Kern ....MMO 2110
A Fine Romance • Smoke Gets In Your Eyes • The Last Time I Saw Paris • The Way You Look Tonight • Yesterdays • The Folks Who Live On The Hill • Make Believe • I'm Old Fashioned • All The Things You Are • They Didn't Believe Me

Vol. 11 - Sing the Songs of Johnny Mercer............................MMO 2111
Come Rain or Come Shine • Charade • The Days of Wine and Roses • Dream • I'm Old Fashioned • I Wanna Be Around • Jeepers Creepers • Moon River • One For My Baby

Vol. 12 - Sing the Songs of Johnny Mercer, Vol. 2 ....MMO 2112
The Autumn Leaves • Fools Rush In • I Remember You • My Shining Hour • Skylark • Tangerine • Too Marvelous For Words • Mr. Meadowlark

Vol. 13 - Sing the Songs of Rodgers & Hart ....MMO 2113
I Didn't Know What Time It Was • My Funny Valentine • Nobody's Heart Belongs To Me • A Ship Without A Sail • Dancing On The Ceiling • It Never Entered My Mind • There's A Small Hotel • Where Or When

Vol. 14 - Sing the Songs of Harry Warren...............................MMO 2114
You'll Never Know • The More I See You • I Wish I Knew • This Is Always • I Had The Craziest Dream • I Only Have Eyes For You • Jeepers Creepers • That's Amore • Serenade In Blue

Music Minus One
50 Executive Boulevard · Elmsford, New York 10523-1325
914-592-1188 · e-mail: info@musicminusone.com
www.musicminusone.com

MMO 2125

ISBN 978-1-941566-25-1